THE LIBRARY OF
AMERICAN
LIVES AND TIMES™

THOMAS PAINE

Common Sense and
Revolutionary
Pamphleteering

Brian McCartin

The Rosen Publishing Group's
PowerPlus Books™
New York

To my loving father James,
My wife and best friend Debbie,
And my amazing and beautiful children
Kellie Rose and Kevin Ryan!

Published in 2002 by The Rosen Publishing Group, Inc.
29 East 21st Street, New York, NY 10010

First Edition

Editor's Note: All quotations have been reproduced as they appeared in the
letters and diaries from which they were borrowed. No correction was made
to the inconsistent spelling that was common during that time period.

Library of Congress Cataloging-in-Publication Data

McCartin, Brian.
  Thomas Paine : common sense and revolutionary pamphleteering / by
Brian McCartin.— 1st ed.
    p. cm. — (The library of American lives and times)
  Includes bibliographical references and index.
  ISBN 0-8239-5729-2 (lib. bdg.)
  1. Paine, Thomas, 1737–1809—Juvenile literature. 2. Political
scientists—Biography—Juvenile literature.
  3. Revolutionaries—Biography—Juvenile literature. [1. Paine, Thomas,
1737—1809. 2. Political scientists. 3. Revolutionaries.]   I. Title.
II. Series.
JC178.V5 M35 2002
320.51'092—dc21

                                                    2001000607

Manufactured in the United States of America

CONTENTS

Introduction

We have it in our Power to begin the World over again!

—Thomas Paine

These revolutionary words from *Common Sense* inspired the American colonists to action, turning a rebellion over taxation into a revolution for freedom.

Fighting between Britain and her American colonies had been going on since April 1775, but rebel leaders had not defined the cause for which they were fighting. Then on January 10, 1776, Thomas Paine published *Common Sense*. This best-selling, forty-seven-page pamphlet defined the cause of America as liberty. It called for the replacement of monarchy with an independent republic founded on the principles of freedom and equality.

Although of humble origins, Paine rose to become one of the most influential political figures and the

---

Opposite: This 1880 painting of Thomas Paine is by Auguste Millière, from an engraving by William Sharp, based on George Romney's 1793 portrait. Paine would become the foremost writer of political pamphlets in the 1700s. As early as the 1500s, pamphleteering was a common way to voice dissent against social or religious injustices. In North America, pre-Revolutionary political unrest stimulated extensive pamphleteering.

best-selling author of the 1700s. English by birth, French by decree, and American by choice, he was a leader in the American and French Revolutions. In his greatest works, including *Common Sense, Rights of Man*, and *The Age of Reason*, Thomas Paine proposed a political and social system based on liberty, justice, and equality. These principles inspired men to fight, and even die, for freedom in America, France, and England. Ultimately these principles have changed the course of modern history.

1. Courage Under Fire

Webster's Dictionary defines courage as "the mental or moral strength to venture, persevere, and withstand danger, fear, or difficulty."

During the eighteenth century, one man fit this description better than all others did. That man was Thomas Paine. With a firm belief in the rights of the individual, Paine challenged the traditional authority of king and church. By writing in support of freedom and truth, Paine became a popular hero to the common man and the number one enemy of those opposed to liberty, equality, and justice for all. Although slandered, threatened, outlawed, and even imprisoned by his enemies, Paine never wavered in his courageous fight for the oppressed.

Thomas Paine's brave fight began with his first publicly acknowledged pamphlet, "The Case of the Officers of the Excise." Paine, himself an excise officer, had been asked to petition for higher wages for excisemen. Unfortunately Paine's petition was unsuccessful. He was soon fired from his job for being absent from his

This cartoon, "Who Wants Me," is by Isaac Cruikshank.
In it Paine is writing titles of his radical works on the scroll.
The artist is criticizing Paine, and writes "Common Nonsense" rather
than "Common Sense" as the title of Paine's most famous work.
He also shows Paine crushing such ideas as "Obedience to the Laws"
and "Morality" underfoot. Despite slanderous and critical works such
as this, Paine continued to write for a cause he knew was just.

work without permission, though many believed it was because of his petition. Ironically, this event forced him to travel to America, where his revolutionary appeal for liberty and justice would help create a new republic.

Thomas Paine's early American writings reflected a growing dislike for the British government. Paine felt that one of the greatest injustices enacted by the British government was the institution of the African slave trade in the colonies. He criticized the government, and the colonists who took part, when he wrote:

> *"That some desperate wretches should be willing to steal and enslave men by violence and murder for gain is rather lamentable than strange. But that many civilized, nay, Christianized people should approve, and be concerned in the savage practice, is surprising. To go to nations with whom there is no war, who have no way provoked, without farther design of conquest, purely to catch inoffensive people, like wild beasts, for slaves, is an height of outrage against humanity and justice. By such wicked and inhuman ways the English are said to enslave towards one hundred thousand yearly."*

Thomas Paine then challenged the colonists to abolish slavery, "How just, how suitable to our crime is the punishment with which providence threatens us?

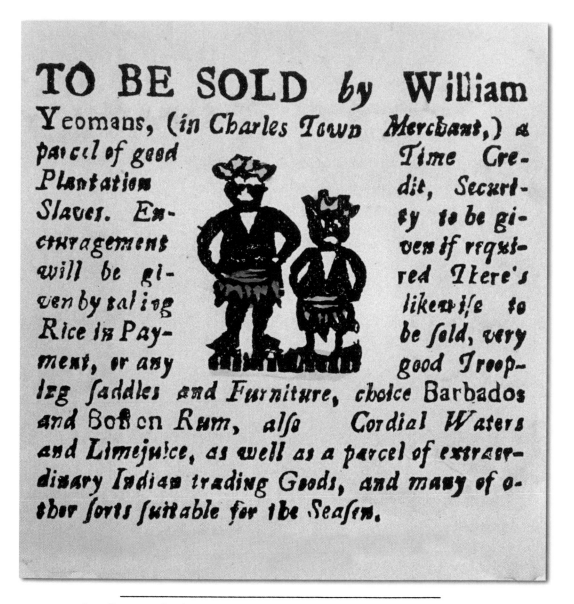

This illustrated advertisement from the 1744 *Charleston Gazette* was advertising the sale of "good Plantation Slaves" along with other items such as rum, cordial waters, and Indian trading goods. It clearly shows that the colonists thought of African slaves as goods to be bought and sold. Thomas Paine felt this thinking was very hypocritical and inhumane and challenged the colonists to abolish the practice of slavery.

We have enslaved multitudes, and shed much innocent blood in doing it; and now are threatened with the same."

Soon after this March 1775 publication, Paine became a founding member of the first abolitionist society, in Philadelphia. Although slavery continued for ninety more years in America, Paine's courageous stand against slavery reflected his developing political philosophy, which linked liberty to equality for all.

The political situation in the colonies in 1775 was confusing and chaotic. Paine used his pen to give Americans a cause. In *Common Sense* he wrote, "The Cause of America is in great measure, the Cause of all Mankind."

After the war, Thomas Paine would fight for the common man once more, this time in Europe. By 1789, France had exploded into revolution. In response, Paine wrote *Rights of Man,* which became the best-selling radical political tract in eighteenth-century England. He became a hero to the people of France and an enemy of the British government.

Paine again came under fire for writing *The Age of Reason*. Challenging religious authority, he wrote, "I believe in the equality of man; and I believe that religious duties consist in doing justice, loving mercy, and endeavoring to make our fellow creatures happy." Returning to America in 1802, Thomas Paine fell under attack by the clergy. These religious leaders joined his political enemies in trying to make America forget one of her most courageous heroes.

Mad Tom's first Practical Essay on the Rights of MAN

This 1797 political cartoon, "Mad Tom's First Practical Essay on the Rights of Man," is by Isaac Cruikshank. Cruikshank commonly criticized Paine's ideas in his cartoons. Despite Cruikshank's criticism, *Rights of Man* sold more than 200,000 copies and would inspire the common people of France to fight for liberty.

Yet the legacy of Thomas Paine endures. As James Monroe writes: "It is unnecessary for me to tell you how much all your countrymen . . . are interested in your welfare. You are considered by them as not only having rendered important services in our own Revolution, but as being on a more extensive scale, the friend of human rights, and a distinguished and able advocate in favor of public liberty."

This is the story of Thomas Paine, whose courage under fire helped to "rescue man from tyranny . . . and enable him to be free."

2. English Born

Who was this man who would inspire two revolutions and bring America into an age in which human rights and dignity have become the standard for which revolutions are fought and by which all nations judge their freedom? His story begins in the small town of Thetford, 75 miles (121 km) north of London, England, in the county of Norfolk. Thetford was a farming community located on the banks of two rivers, the Thet and Little Ouse. With its small manufacturing and trade economy, Thetford served as a market town and trading center for the surrounding towns and villages.

This is the house in Thetford, England, in which Thomas Paine was born.

In the year of Paine's birth, Thetford's small population of two thousand people included a wide range of social classes. Wealthy lawyers and merchants formed the upper level of an expanding middle class, and shopkeepers and artisans formed its lower middle class. For

most of the eighteenth century, the number of poor in Thetford, England, remained low despite the labor unrest and food riots spreading throughout the rest of the country. The estates of the wealthy aristocracy and landed gentry dominated the surrounding countryside. At a time when land meant wealth and wealth

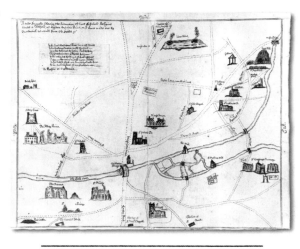

This is an eighteenth-century map of Thetford, drawn by Thomas Martin.

meant power, the landowning nobles and untitled country squires in England were members of a new ruling class that rose to power at the end of the seventeenth century.

Like many rural towns and villages in the England of Paine's childhood, Thetford was under the control of a wealthy aristocrat. Through a system of patronage and bribery, wealthy nobles exercised total control over towns and boroughs throughout the English countryside. As part of this "rotten borough" system of government, Thetford and several other small villages fell under the control of the Duke of Grafton. With an

Opposite: This is a 1762 portrait of Augustus Henry Fitzroy, third Duke of Grafton, by Pompeo Batoni. Fitzroy lived from 1735 to 1811 and was duke during the time Thomas Paine was growing up in Thetford.

estate almost 40 miles (64 km) in circumference, the Grafton family maintained influence over the political and social affairs of Thetford for generations.

By providing jobs, buying votes, and choosing their districts' representatives to the House of Commons, the Duke and his fellow nobles were able to control Parliament for most of the eighteenth century. As members of Parliament's ruling political party, known as the Whigs or antiroyalist party, men like the Duke had risen to power following the religious and political wars in seventeenth-century England.

By the end of the seventeenth century, England's wars for colonial trade had established a global trading empire. By the 1700s, the increase in wealth from colonial trade had fueled England's scientific and industrial revolutions, which would take firm hold by the late 1700s. With the world's most powerful navy patrolling the oceans and protecting her empire, Britain influenced events around the world. As the power and wealth of Britain increased during the eighteenth century, so did a sense of nationalism. All classes of Englishmen and women took pride in their nation's political system, military power, and scientific inventions.

Yet in 1737, the year of Paine's birth, the majority of Englishmen could not participate in government. Men without property or who earned less than an annual income of forty shillings could not vote or hold office.

As the representative body of the English government, Parliament did little for the common man. The Whig ruling class denied representation to the majority of English citizens by controlling the House of Lords through inheritance and the House of Commons through patronage and bribery. Out of a population of five million Englishmen, only six thousand could vote!

During Thomas Paine's childhood, economic conditions for the lower classes of English society grew steadily worse. Labor unrest, due to poor working conditions, and food riots, caused by food shortages, spread throughout England. Cities became overcrowded with the rural poor and dispossessed. Residents of these cities

The English Parliament was formed during the reign of Edward I from 1272-1307. At first Parliament's duty was to advise the king and rubber-stamp his proposals, but by the fourteenth century, Parliament was making laws on its own without royal consent. By the seventeenth century, Parliament reached the height of its powers, becoming the chief law-making body in the nation and taking away most royal power. Parliament also was split into two branches. It included the House of Lords and the House of Commons, which served as models for the U. S. Senate and House of Representatives.

responded to increasing political and social injustices through resistance, protests, and riots.

Fearing a return to the political and social unrest of the previous century, both the English government and Anglican Church tried to prevent the resistance through various methods. Both the state and the Anglican Church expended a great deal of energy trying to convince the lower classes, through propaganda, that English society was better and freer than the societies of other European nations. The great myth that all freeborn Englishmen were equal before the law would even make its way to British America in the 1700s. Failing to keep law and order this way, Parliament passed into law almost two hundred capital crimes in order to maintain "liberty and property" for the English ruling classes. For committing such minor offenses as stealing bread, women and children were sent to the gallows. While the lower classes suffered oppression and social injustice, wealth and power acquired through war and trade encouraged the ruling classes to pursue scientific progress, industrial development, and the establishment of a world empire. This was England in the year of Thomas Paine's birth.

3. Understanding the Nature of Things

Here lies the body of John Crow,
Who once was high but now is low;
Ye brother crows take warning all,
For as you rise, so must you fall.

Written when he was eight years old, this dedication to a pet crow was an early expression of Thomas Paine's unique insight into the nature of things. Exposed to injustice and inequality almost from birth, young Thomas was as familiar with the arrogance of crows toward smaller, less powerful birds as he was with the arrogance of the wealthy and powerful toward the suffering lower classes. This simple yet profound realization about equality and justice was a major theme that carried through all of Paine's future writings.

His interest in understanding the nature of things began early in Paine's life. Born in a section of town called the Wilderness, Paine lived in a cottage overlooking Gallows Hill, an execution site where criminals were hung for their crimes. In the spring of each year, Thetford hosted the civil and criminal court sessions for the county of Norfolk. Every March hundreds of visitors from the surrounding towns swelled Thetford's inns and

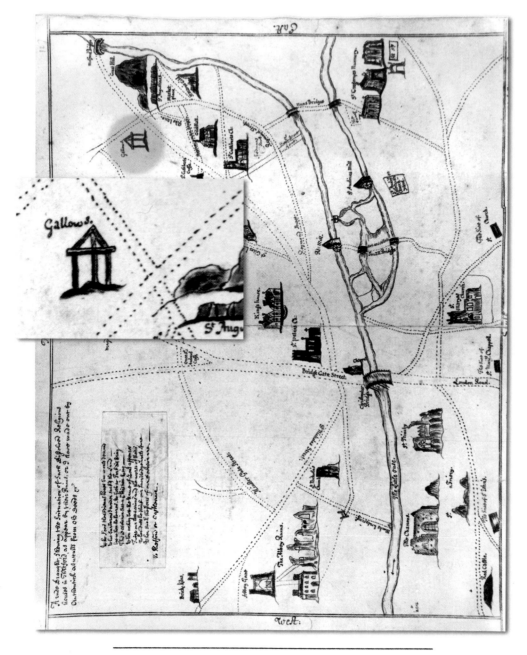

This Thetford map was drawn by Thomas Martin in the 1700s. The boxed inset shows the gallows that Thomas Paine could see from his window. Britain's use of the death penalty reached its peak in the 1700s, when the list of crimes punishable by death was enlarged to over 200 offenses, including stealing the value of five shillings and sending threatening letters. Starting in the 1820s, this "bloody code" was gradually repealed. By 1861, murder was the only crime punishable by death.

taverns to see this spectacle of state justice. Most criminal cases were about the stealing of food, money, or property by the poor. Most of these crimes were committed out of need and desperation. Nevertheless, in a society ruled by the wealthy and in which wealth was measured by property, such property, no matter how small, was protected at all costs. Punishments for these crimes included hanging, exile, the pillory, whipping, or imprisonment. Meanwhile, if the wealthy committed crimes, even murder, they were often just fined.

For the first nineteen springs of his life, Thomas Paine was an eyewitness to the brutality and injustice

Collection of the New-York Historical Society, Negative Number 48817

This 1775 engraving is titled *A Hanging in Cambridge, Mass., 1755.* The methods of punishment, such as hanging, that Thomas Paine witnessed while growing up were brought to America by the colonists. Paine would work his whole life to change the brutal and unjust practices he saw used by governments wherever he went.

Tom Paine's Nightly Pest, by James Gillray, was published in London by H. Humphrey in 1792. Because of his radical ideas, Paine was hated and feared by many conservative politicians through-out his life. Here Paine fears he will be sent to the gallows, just as many of the people he saw growing up were, for his ideas. He lies on a pillow wrapped in the American flag and the curtains have fleur-de-lis on them as a symbol of France.

executed by the state in the name of English law. He saw the local prison from his house, and, every year on execution day, he saw the prisoners as they marched up Gallows Hill with their hands and feet shackled. He saw them with their eyes covered by black handkerchiefs as their bodies fell through the opening scaffold floor. He saw their dying bodies dangle in the cold, spring air for the customary hour. The injustice and brutality of English law made a strong impression on his young mind and gave him an early understanding of the nature of power and wealth and the government's use of brutality and injustice to maintain its power. Paine expressed this understanding years later when he wrote:

> *"When, in countries that are called civilised, we see age going to the workhouse and youth to the gallows, something must be wrong in the system of government. It would seem, by the exterior appearance of such countries, that all was happiness; but there lies hidden from the eye of common observation, a mass of wretchedness, that has scarcely any other chance, than to expire in poverty or infamy. Its entrance into life is marked with the presage of its fate; and until this is remedied, it is in vain to punish.*
>
> *Civil government does not exist in executions; but in making such provision for the instruction of youth and the support of age. Instead of this, the resources of a country are lavished upon kings, upon courts, upon hirelings, impostors and prostitutes; and even the poor themselves, with all their wants upon them, are compelled to support the fraud that oppresses them. Why is it that scarcely any are executed but the poor?"*

Closer to home, Paine witnessed another form of injustice, religious intolerance. Francis Cocke, Thomas's mother, was the daughter of a middle-class lawyer and member of the Anglican State Church. In 1734, she married Joseph Pain, the son of a Quaker shoemaker. Marrying outside of one's class and religion was unusual in a century when class and church membership determined one's rights. Yet these differences in social class and religion did not deter the couple, and after almost three years of marriage, Francis Pain gave birth to Thomas on January 29, 1737. (Thomas added the "e" to his last name after going to America.) The following year, a daughter, Elizabeth, was born to the couple but died within a year.

Thomas grew up as an only child in a mixed-religious home. Baptized and confirmed an Anglican, he learned the Bible and catechism at home, school, and church. However, Thomas grew to doubt a church that scared him with its sermons of a vengeful God and disappointed him with its intolerance toward the Quakers in Thetford. This early lesson in the power of the established church later influenced Thomas to write on behalf of freedom of religion and the separation of church and state.

Although given freedom to worship by the Toleration Act of 1689, as a religious minority Quakers were unable to vote or hold office in eighteenth-century England. Founded and led by George Fox and later by William Penn, Quakers are still practicing their religion today. In Thomas Paine's time, however, their beliefs seemed

This engraved portrait of George Fox is based on a painting by S. Chinn. Fox lived from 1624 to 1691.

strange to other people. Quakers opposed formal religion, religious authority, and church taxes. Along with their belief in equality and a strong moral stance against slavery, war, and capital punishment, Quakers also believed in one's "inner light." They felt that God dwelled in every person, and therefore the church and clergy were unnecessary. Persecuted by the established church, Quakers formed tight-knit groups and practiced mutual aid by taking care of their poorer members. Learning these Quaker principles from his father, Thomas developed a strong sense of equality and the strength of community action.

At the age of seven, Thomas began his formal education at the Thetford Grammar School, near his house. Founded two centuries earlier, the Puritan-run school was free to the children of freeborn Englishmen in Thetford. As the son of a freeman, Thomas attended the school for the next six years. Forbidden by the Quakers to learn the official language of the state and church, Joseph Pain prevented his son from learning Latin in school. Limited in his education to arithmetic, science, accounting, and English, Thomas excelled at

This is a nineteenth-century engraving of Thetford Grammar School. The school, still in existence today, was first formed in 631, but a plaque on its wall reads: "This school is one of the oldest in the country. It was refounded by Sir Richard Fulmerston in 1566. Thomas Paine was a pupil here from 1744 to 1749."

mathematics and had a strong interest in science and poetry. Hearing stories of adventures on the high seas and reading a history of Virginia stirred his curious nature and adventurous spirit. Nonetheless, without Latin, his career choices were limited. In 1750, at age thirteen, Thomas left school to begin serving as an apprentice to his father.

Seven years was the standard term of apprenticeship for most trades, and Joseph Pain's staymaking trade was no different. Making stays for ships' masts had been the primary occupation of staymakers for centuries. Another type of staymaking during the eighteenth century was a form of corset making. Whether Joseph was the type of staymaker that made stays for ships or stays for corsets is still a matter of controversy. We do know, however, that after six years as an apprentice staymaker, an occupation imposed more by his social class and limited formal education than by personal choice, Thomas Paine left home. Bored and impatient with life in a small town, Thomas left for London. Here he would take his next step on a lifelong journey to understand the nature of things.

This undated engraving shows men making stays for the masts of ships. It is unclear whether Thomas Paine's father was the maker of stays for ships or for corsets. In shipbuilding, stays were large, strong ropes used to support masts and keep them from moving.

4. The Adventure Begins

At age nineteen, Thomas was tall with dark hair, bright eyes, and the strong, skilled hands of an artisan. For the previous six years, Thomas had worked closely with his father to learn the skills of the staymaking craft. During their long hours together, Thomas listened as Joseph spoke of the Quakers' egalitarian beliefs and the story of their religious struggles in the seventeenth century. Thomas had grown close to his father during those years. Influenced by Joseph's Quaker values, Thomas later wrote, "My father being of the Quaker profession, it was my good fortune to have an exceedingly good moral education, and a tolerable stock of learning."

However, with a limited market for stays in Thetford, Thomas realized that he would have to leave his father's shop in order to find work and complete the next stage of his training as a journeyman staymaker. Thomas Paine decided to go to London. Spurred on by his readings of Daniel Defoe's *Robinson Crusoe* and Jonathan Swift's *Gulliver's Travels*, Thomas Paine left home and set out on an adventure that would change the world.

As the capital of the British Empire, London must have seemed exotic and a bit overwhelming to Thomas when he arrived in 1756. With a population of six hundred thousand people and a diversity of goods from around the world, London and its cobblestone streets rang with the sound of cart wheels, horses' hooves, and peddlers selling everything from newspapers to rabbits.

Through a connection of his father's, Thomas secured a room and a position as a journeyman staymaker with John Morris. Morris was a master artisan who worked in the Covent Garden section of London. Thomas's location placed him near the city's most infamous brothels as well as its taverns, coffeehouses, and theaters. With dogfights, fistfights, and pickpockets, the noise, violence, and crime of the area stimulated Paine's curiosity. However, long hours of work and dependence on his master did little to satisfy his desire for independence and adventure. Little did Paine know that events in America already were beginning to shape his destiny.

By 1756, fighting over territorial rights between France and England in the American colonies had escalated into the Seven Years' War in Europe, called the French and Indian War (1754–1763) in America. Even before Paine's arrival, war-fever and patriotism had

Following Spread: This is a seventeenth-century map of London by Georgius Braun. Notice the bustling streets as well as the wealthy lords and ladies on the hillside, overseeing the activity. London during Thomas Paine's time would have been similarly busy.

ISSIMI AN.
...ETROPOLIS

The Spitel fields.

y⁰ Gomnfrowders P.

Pattern Gate

THE TOWRE

Bette hows

STILLIARDS) Hansa, Gothica dictio, conuentum, vel congregationem fin. nan-
tarum ciuitatum eſt cõfœderata Societas, tum ob præſita Regibus, ac Ducib.
cia: tum ob securam terra marique mercatura traſtationem, tum deniq̃; a
quillam Rerumpub. pacem, & ad modeſam adoleſcentum inſtitutionem conſe-
dam, inſtituta: plurimor. Regum, ac Principum, maximè Angliæ, Galliæ, Dan.
Magnæ Moſcouiæ, nec non Flandriæ, ac Brabantiæ Ducum priuilegijs, ac immu-
tatib. exornata fuit. Habet ea quatuor Emporia, (untores quidam vocant, in q̃
ciuitatum negotiatores reſident. ſuaſq̃; mercatus excercent. Hor. alterum hẽ-
ni, domeſtica œconomia nitet, habens domum Gildehalla Teutonica quã vulgo Stilhard.

Cum Priuilegio.

This undated engraving shows the defeat of General Braddock in the French and Indian War. Edward Braddock lived from 1695 to 1755. He was a Scottish soldier in command of British forces in America during the French and Indian War. He was wounded on his way to attack Fort Dusquesne, and he died on July 9, 1755.

been spreading throughout London. While living in the city, Paine read advertisements for seamen to serve on British privateers. Unlike pirate ships, privateers were privately owned ships commissioned by the crown to pursue and capture enemy vessels and their cargoes. After auctioning off the captured vessel and its cargo, the captain and crew shared the profits. Privateering was a means for men and boys from the lower classes to serve their country and make money.

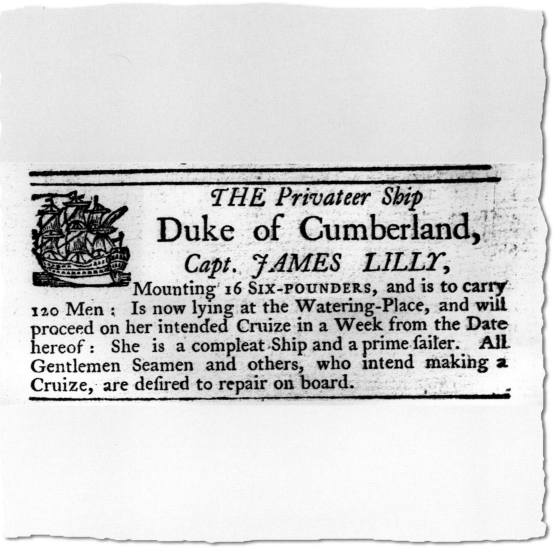

THE Privateer Ship
Duke of Cumberland,
Capt. JAMES LILLY,
Mounting 16 SIX-POUNDERS, and is to carry 120 Men : Is now lying at the Watering-Place, and will proceed on her intended Cruize in a Week from the Date hereof : She is a compleat Ship and a prime failer. All Gentlemen Seamen and others, who intend making a Cruize, are defired to repair on board.

Collection of the New-York Historical Society, Negative Number 49971

This privateer advertisement was printed in the *New York Mercury* on December 4, 1758, during the Seven Years' War. Ads requesting sailors to join a ship's crew and help in the war effort were typical of what Thomas Paine was reading in newspapers around London.

This 1797 engraving shows two young sailors sitting on either side of a painting titled *The Desperate Action Between the* Terrible *and* Vengeance. Thomas Paine had signed on to the crew of the privateer *Terrible*, but luckily his father convinced him not to go. Many people died during the battle scene depicted above.

In the fall of 1756, feeling "raw and adventurous," Thomas Paine signed on to a privateer ship called the *Terrible*, captained by William Death. Somehow hearing of his son's intentions, Joseph Pain convinced Thomas not to ship off. Fortunately for Paine, he listened. Over the next few weeks, Paine read in the newspapers about the great battle between the *Terrible* and a French privateer, the *Vengeance*. Paine later would recall how the *Terrible* "stood the hottest engagement of the war." The ship lost more than 150 crewmen, including Captain Death. With his father's "affectionate and moral remonstrance," soon wearing off, Thomas signed up once more. This time he sailed on the *King of Prussia*, with Captain Menzies.

Life at sea was hard. Even if they didn't have to fight other ships, seamen had to put up with bad food, dirty water, vermin, and diseases like pneumonia and scurvy. Yet the pay could be up to 60 pounds a year, more than double what Joseph Pain made annually as a staymaker. Nonetheless, when the *King of Prussia* completed her successful cruise with nine seized ships, Paine ended his tour of duty as a privateer. Having seen enough of blood and death, Thomas Paine was then ready to use the money he had made to continue his self-education and prepare for his next adventure.

5. A Journeyman's Search

Arriving back in London in August 1757, stimulated by his adventures at sea, Thomas was ready to make another career change. The lessons he had learned about ships and astronomy as a seaman encouraged Paine to pursue his interest in science. Living off the wages he had earned as a privateer, Thomas moved back to Covent Garden and became a professional student. Browsing London bookstores and devouring newspapers, pamphlets, and broadsides, Paine received his formal introduction to the world of eighteenth-century science and philosophy when he attended London's Royal Society.

This illustration shows the coat of arms of London's Royal Society.

Drawn to the scientific lectures at the Royal Society, Paine later recalled, "The natural bent of my mind was to science. As soon as I was able, I purchased a pair of globes, and attended the

Benjamin Martin was a leading scientist of the 1700s. Among other things, he wrote *Grammar of the Philosophical Sciences*.

philosophical lectures of Martin and Ferguson." Benjamin Martin and James Ferguson were part of the scientific revolution in England, a revolution that began in the previous century when Isaac Newton discovered the universal laws of gravity. Newton and his followers believed that laws governing the universe operated in the human world, as well.

By understanding these natural laws through reason and scientific inquiry, men could develop a government that would improve and reform society. As the center of expression for these new ideas, the Royal Society examined topics that ranged from Newton's philosophy to the behavior of comets, the reflection of light, properties of air, and phases of the Moon. Lectures at the society attracted large groups of self-educated shopkeepers and artisans, including many who rejected the traditional notions of the power of the state and church.

Isaac Newton, a great scientist, lived from 1642 to 1727. He joined the Royal Society in 1672.

Paine's exposure to these ideas not only aroused his passion for science but introduced him to new political ideas that equated science and reason with liberty. These ideas, which helped create the scientific and industrial revolutions in England, later would threaten the British ruling class, whose power and wealth came at the expense of the common man. As the levels of poverty and hopelessness increased among the lower classes, the newly self-educated and politically aware working-class shopkeepers and artisans demanded political reform.

A childhood filled with the experiences of public hangings by the state, political corruption by the aristocracy, and religious bigotry by the state church already had made Thomas critical of the power of state and church. With his recent adventures at sea and lessons in science and philosophy at the Royal Society, Paine joined a growing movement of thinkers who passionately believed that through reason and science men could create a better world. Over the next several years, Paine further developed his political and social ideas from a variety of influences. The first came when he ran out of money and decided to leave London in search of work.

After briefly working again as a journeyman staymaker in Dover, Paine moved to Sandwich by 1759 and set up his own small shop as a master staymaker. During his time there, Paine was influenced by the Methodist movement under the leadership of John Wesley. The Methodist religion offered hope to the masses by saying

This twentieth-century photograph shows the street where Thomas Paine set up his staymaking shop in Sandwich, England, in 1759. Paine would remain in Sandwich for only a short time before he moved to Margate with his wife, Mary Lambert Paine.

that all who practiced self-discipline and good works could achieve salvation. Encouraging literacy and education for the common man, Methodist thinking influenced Paine's developing sense of egalitarianism.

Sandwich also provided Thomas with his first love, Mary Lambert. They were married in the fall of 1759, and soon Mary was pregnant. The couple left town following Mary's pregnancy and Thomas began another business in the seacoast town of Margate. Unfortunately, Paine's happiness did not last. Falling ill during childbirth, Mary died, as did the child, in the summer of 1760. Devastated by his loss, the twenty-three-year-old Paine was sad, lonely, and confused. Yet, determined to make another change in his life, he recalled Mary's conversations regarding her father's occupation as an exciseman. The English excise officers assessed and collected taxes on goods such as alcohol and tobacco, and patrolled the shoreline for smuggling. Although working as an exciseman was a low-paying and sometimes dangerous job, Paine's strong desire for change prompted him to seek his parents' support so he could learn to become one.

Shortly after his wife's death, Thomas Paine returned to Thetford to study for the required entrance examinations. Finally gaining an appointment as an exciseman in late 1762, Paine spent the next few years working in small towns. Disappointed with the corruption he saw, Paine eventually left the excise office. Over the next few years, Paine worked as an artisan and then as a teacher in London. During this time, Paine witnessed London's economic and political unrest, caused by food shortages, unemployment, the government crackdown on labor protests, and newspaper articles critical of the king and his ministers. Paine also reacquainted himself with James Ferguson and met other members of the Royal Society, including Benjamin Franklin.

Recalling this time in his life, Paine remarked: "Here I derived considerable information; indeed I have seldom passed five minutes of my life, however circumstanced, in

Charles Willson Peale painted this portrait of Benjamin Franklin in 1789. It is oil on canvas.

Benjamin Franklin was one of the most influential leaders during America's rise from a colony to a new nation. Franklin was an author, diplomat, and statesman. He was instrumental in helping to write the Declaration of Independence, in securing help from France during the Revolution, and in negotiating the treaty with Great Britain, ending the war. Franklin also contributed to the fabric of daily life in America. He invented the lightning rod and bifocal eyeglasses, while also founding the first library, fire department, and insurance company in the United States.

which I did not acquire some knowledge." Indeed, now thirty years old, Paine had acquired a substantial understanding of political oppression, religious intolerance, and the need for justice and liberty. The next step in formalizing Paine's political and social principles would come through his role as a community leader and labor activist in Lewes, England. Paine petitioned the government for reinstatement as an exciseman in 1767. By 1768, he was again an excise officer, this time in Lewes.

Between 1768 and 1774, Thomas Paine became an active member in the community. In 1771, he married Elizabeth Ollive, the daughter of a prominent local official. Paine eventually took over the Ollive family business but kept his job as an exciseman. As the leading political debater in the local tavern known as the White Hart Inn, Paine developed a reputation as a "shrewd and sensible fellow with a depth of political knowledge."

Aside from Paine's local reputation, his fellow excisemen outside of Lewes also knew Thomas Paine as a man skilled with words. With discontent growing over low wages and hazardous working conditions, the nation's excisemen commissioned Paine to write a formal petition to Parliament requesting a salary increase. In the summer of 1772, Thomas Paine authored his first public pamphlet, entitled, "The Case of the Officers of the Excise." Paine spent the next several months in London lobbying members of Parliament with his petition. In his first public argument against poverty, Paine stressed that

*One of the club members
from the White Hart Inn dubbed Paine
"General of the Headstrong Club,"
meaning that Thomas Paine was
always willing to speak his mind
and stick to his opinions. For Paine's vigorous
defense of liberty and justice, the club member
wrote the following ode:*

"Immortal PAINE! While mighty reasoners jar,
We crown thee General of the Headstrong War;
Thy logic vanquish'd error, and thy mind
No bounds, but those of right and truth, confined.
Thy soul of fire must sure ascend the sky,
Immortal PAINE, thy fame can never die;
For men like thee their names must ever save
From the black edicts of the tyrant grave."

it bred frustration, complacency, and hopelessness in the people. Paine argued that higher salaries were needed to keep excisemen from poverty and possible corruption. "Poverty," Paine wrote, "in defiance of principle, begets a degree of meanness that will stoop to almost anything. . . . Nothing, tends to a greater corruption of manners and principles than a too great distress of circumstances." He also wrote, "The continuance of work, the strictness of the duty, and the poverty of the salary, soon beget negligence and indifference: the course continues for a while, the revenue suffers, and the officer is discharged; the vacancy is soon filled up, new ones arise to produce the same mischief and share the same fate."

Although unsuccessful, Paine had attempted to use logic and morality as the foundation of justice. This would become the cornerstone of all Paine's future work.

Upon Paine's return to Lewes in 1773, the family business and his marriage to Elizabeth began to fall apart. The following year, Paine received a dismissal notice from the excise office and agreed to separate from his wife. Giving her all of their belongings, Thomas Paine left Lewes and went to London. There he spent time with Benjamin Franklin, who recommended that he sail to America. In autumn 1774, Paine sailed for America on the *London Packet* with little more than his letters of introduction from Franklin and a suitcase of clothes. Little did he know that his quest for a new beginning in America would result in America's new beginning.

6. A Crisis in the Colonies

Thomas Paine's revolutionary career in America almost ended before it began. Departing on the *London Packet* in late September 1774, Paine and most of the ship's passengers were stricken by an epidemic of typhus during their two-month-long voyage. More dead than alive when he arrived in Philadelphia in November, Thomas Paine had to be carried off the ship on a stretcher. Fortunately for Paine, his friendship with Philadelphia's great Franklin brought him to the attention of Dr. John Kearsley, who attended to him for the next six weeks. Fully recovered by the following January, Paine had letters of recommendation from Franklin to Richard Bache to help him obtain employment as a tutor. Taking advantage of this opportunity, Paine took up rooms near the waterfront and began to explore his new home in America.

By the time of Paine's arrival, the American colonies were thriving, dynamic, and rebellious. A population of three million included a variety of European nationalities and about 750,000 African slaves. The majority of

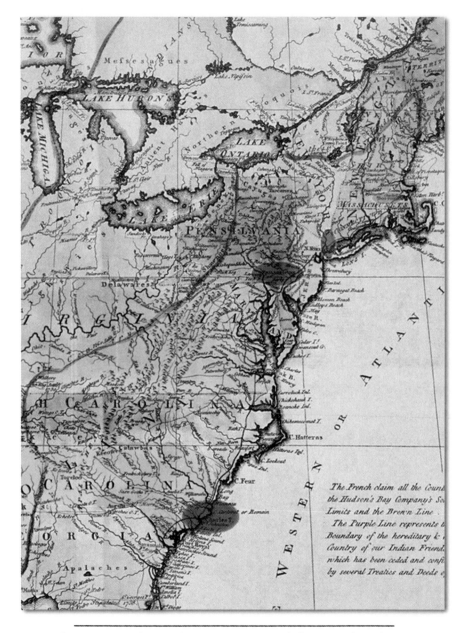

This is an eighteenth-century map of the British colonies
as they appeared when Paine arrived in America. The major
seaports that were the centers of trade in the colonies are
highlighted: Boston is in a blue oval; New York is in an orange
one; Philadelphia, a purple; and Charleston is in a red oval.

colonists lived in the countryside, but trade and sea-ports had created several major urban centers by the 1770s. New York, Boston, Philadelphia, and Charleston had become major commercial centers linking the colonies to England, Europe, and the rest of the world.

In the 1700s, the image of America as a land of opportunity, where merit and not class determined one's limits, was popular among most Englishmen, including Paine. Recalling an early interest in America, he wrote, "I happened when a schoolboy to pick up a pleasing natural history of Virginia, and my inclination from that day of seeing the western side of the Atlantic never left me."

In many ways, the British colonies in America must have seemed much like England to Paine. In the colonies, criminal justice was cruel, capital crimes were many, and women still were being punished for witchcraft. Popular forms of entertainment in both countries included cockfighting, gambling, and drinking in taverns or spending time in coffeehouses. In the colonies as in England, property determined voting rights. Like their British counterparts, the lower classes in America were excluded from political participation and sometimes resorted to mob actions to voice their complaints. The colonies in America had replaced English aristocracy with a colonial ruling class of southern planters, northern landlords, and wealthy merchants. Forming the political and social leadership of colonial America, these ruling elite, like their English cousins, enjoyed English liberties while denying those liberties to others. Below yet closely connected to this ruling class, as in England, were the middle-class lawyers and clergy, followed by the working-class shopkeepers and artisans, and then by farmers, laborers, and the poor. Yet significant differences did exist between Britain and her American colonies.

Wealth was more widely dispersed in America than in England, and with the majority of white males being property owners with voting rights, America was far more democratic. Religious diversity in colonial America created a more tolerant attitude throughout the colonies. With a relatively free press, there was an abundance of newspapers, pamphlets, and broadsides, and access to scientific and political literature. Therefore, Americans had the highest literacy rate in the eighteenth-century world. Loyalty to their king and pride in their English liberties gave the diverse colonies a common bond between themselves and the mother country. However, suspicious of a corrupt Parliament, American colonists began to resist Parliament's attempt to increase its control over the colonies. Beginning in the previous decade, colonial resistance had escalated into open rebellion by the time of Paine's arrival in Philadelphia in late 1774. Soon finding himself at the center of the American resistance movement, he later confessed to Franklin, "I thought it very hard to have the country set on fire about my ears almost the moment I got into it." Barely one year later, Paine's own inflammatory words in *Common Sense* would light the torch that would show the way to American freedom.

Following her triumph over the French in the Seven Years' War in Europe (1756–1763) and the French and Indian War in America, Britain controlled vast amounts of territory in North America, including Canada and lands west of the Appalachian Mountains. The expense of this war had drained the British treasury and had forced the government to raise taxes at home and abroad. To this end, King George III and his chief finance minister, George Grenville, decided that the American colonists should assume the cost for the administration and protection of the colonies. Therefore, the British parliament called for increased regulation and taxation of her American colonies. Over the next ten years, Parliament enacted a series of unpopular and, to many colonists, unfair acts that included: the Proclamation of 1763, the Sugar Act of 1764, the Stamp and Quartering Acts of 1765, the Declaratory Act of 1766, the Townshend Acts of 1767, the Tea Act of 1773, and the Coercive Acts of 1774. These actions by the British government seemed perfectly legal to the king and his ministers. They believed that the government had the authority to make laws for all English citizens, including those in the colonies. However, many American colonists disagreed and began a resistance movement.

Beginning in 1765, colonial leaders were the first to protest these new restrictions and taxes by Parliament.

This cartoon was published in a London paper on the day King George III repealed the Stamp Act. The cartoon made fun of George Grenville, here called George Stamper, and his supporters for this and other unpopular taxes. Grenville carries a small coffin holding his "child," the Stamp Act.

Using speeches, pamphlets, newspapers, and broadsides, men like Sam Adams, James Otis, and John Dickinson wrote and spoke passionately against British tyranny. These actions soon aroused popular sentiment, and the common masses gathered in street protests, hung figures in effigy, and even attacked British officials and property. As Parliament continued its policy of taxation, American resistance grew from protests and boycotts to violence. In 1770, a confrontation known as the Boston Massacre broke out between British soldiers and a Boston crowd. It ended in five colonists' deaths. As the resistance escalated, colonial leaders organized patriot groups like the Sons of Liberty. They also established communication between the colonies through groups called Committees of Correspondence. On the night of December 16, 1773, men disguised as Native Americans destroyed a large shipment of British tea. This act, known as the Boston Tea Party, resulted in a new set of parliamentary laws called the Coercive, or Intolerable, Acts. By clos-

This now-famous engraving was created by Paul Revere in 1770, to commemorate the event that became known as the Boston Massacre and to stir up the colonists against British soldiers in Boston.

ing Boston Harbor and putting the colony of Massachusetts under military control, the British government forced the colonists into action.

By September 1774, colonial leaders had formed the First Continental Congress. With the exception of Georgia, all the colonies sent delegates to Philadelphia to discuss what their course of action should be. Agreeing on a continental boycott of all British goods, they issued Parliament a declaration of grievances, or complaints, and began to arm and train their colonial militias.

7. The Power of Revolutionary Prose

Arriving in Philadelphia shortly after the First Continental Congress ended, Thomas Paine found himself at the center of the American resistance movement. Founded in the previous century by the Quaker William Penn, Pennsylvania had served as a haven for Quakers from persecution in England. Philadelphia, with its red brick houses, cobblestone streets, and population of thirty thousand people, was Pennsylvania's leading city. It also was America's busiest seaport. Thomas Paine felt at home in this City of Brotherly Love where Catholics, Anglicans, Quakers, and Jews all lived peaceably. Stimulated by the recent meeting of the Continental Congress, Philadelphia's political atmosphere was charged. Talk of "liberty" and "no taxation without representation" was heard both in the coffeehouses and in the taverns, where working-class citizens were beginning to demand the right of political participation. Renting rooms near the waterfront, Paine was exposed daily to the city's slave market. He later mentioned the irony of American colonists asking for freedom yet denying it to those

Collection of the New-York Historical Society, Negative Number 29401

This 1799 engraving of Philadelphia in the late eighteenth century was done by W. Birch. As America's busiest seaport at the time, Philadelphia was the logical center of political activities, as well. Thomas Paine was in the right place to make an impact on the events that were taking shape in the late 1700s in America.

whom they enslaved. His rooms were also next to Robert Aitken's bookstore on Front Street, where he went to read about the latest scientific ideas. During one of his visits to the bookstore, Paine was inclined to show Aitken several of his unpublished essays and poems. Impressed by Paine's work, Aitken offered him a position with his new journal, *Pennsylvania Magazine*.

Thomas Paine took the position. Over the next several months, Paine's unique style of writing and his controversial articles dramatically increased the circulation of the magazine. Challenging the institution of slavery and supporting justice for woman put Paine among the earliest American writers to advocate equality for slaves and women. However, when fighting between the colonial patriots and British Regulars broke out at Lexington and Concord in the spring of 1775, Thomas Paine began to focus on the need for independence. Reflecting on the "shot heard 'round the world," Paine wrote: "No man was a warmer wisher for a reconciliation than myself, before the fatal nineteenth of April, 1775, but the moment the event of that day was made known, I rejected the hardened, sullen-tempered Pharaoh of England for ever; and disdain the wretch, that with the pretended title of FATHER OF HIS PEOPLE can unfeelingly hear of their slaughter, and composedly sleep with their blood upon his soul."

For the next eight months, Paine's literary style, which embraced large audiences, and his commitment to independence brought him to the attention of the Continental Congress. In July 1775, Paine argued that words alone could no longer defend American liberty from British tyranny: "I am thus far a Quaker, that I would gladly agree with all the world to lay aside the use of arms, and settle matters by negotiation; but unless the whole will, the matter ends and I take up my musket."

Encouraged by Benjamin Rush and other leaders in the Continental Congress, Thomas Paine began work on *Common Sense* in the fall of 1775.

By the end of 1775, the American resistance movement, over taxation and the colonists' rights, was turning into a colonial war. The British king already had declared that "the New England governments are in a state of rebellion, blows must decide," and had the British fleet surround Boston. Fighting soon spread into Canada and the South when the British government refused a petition by Congress to negotiate. Yet the leaders of the Second Continental Congress feared the consequences of independence. They were afraid that with independence might come chaos, mob rule, and loss of their property and power, and they still hoped for reconciliation. Congress refused to speak of independence even as they prepared for war. These actions provoked Paine to write, "The present state of America is truly alarming . . . Legislation without law; wisdom without a plan; a constitution without a name; and, what is strangely astonishing, perfect independence contending for dependence."

Believing that the message was more important than personal recognition, Thomas Paine's *Common Sense* was originally signed "Written by an Englishman." Printed and published by Robert Bell in Philadelphia on January 10, 1776, the first edition of *Common Sense*, a stitched forty-seven-page pamphlet, sold out within two weeks. The impact of this document on American liberty and democratic government was world shattering. Never has any single work of American political literature equaled either the number circulated or impact of *Common Sense*.

One hundred fifty thousand copies (equivalent to fifteen million copies today) were circulating within three months of its publication, with estimates as high as five hundred thousand by the end of the year. Besides being America's greatest best-seller, it also became one throughout Europe. John Adams later recalled, "*Common Sense* was received in France and Europe with Rapture."

For almost a year, Thomas Paine had been hearing the colonial arguments over the conflict with Britain. From the working-class taverns to the coffeehouses of the upper class, all agreed that changes had to come! Understanding the nature of the American colonists, Paine appealed to their independent spirit, love of liberty, and desire for change when he wrote, "O ye that love mankind! Ye that dare oppose, not only the tyranny, but the tyrant, stand forth! Every spot of the old world is overrun with oppression. Freedom hath been hunted round the globe. Asia, and Africa, have long expelled her. —Europe regards her like a stranger, and England hath given her warning to depart. O! receive the fugitive, and prepare in time an asylum for mankind."

With these words, Thomas Paine offered his vision of America to the colonists. For more than two centuries, the revolutionary prose of *Common Sense* has identified America as the land of liberty and as a sanctuary for those who seek freedom and justice. Founded on the principles of liberty, justice, and equality, America, Paine believed, would be the birthplace of a new world. Once established, Paine believed that the American Empire of Liberty would then spread its principles around the world. However, before there could be an American republic, Thomas Paine had to convince the colonists and their leaders of the need for independence from Great Britain.

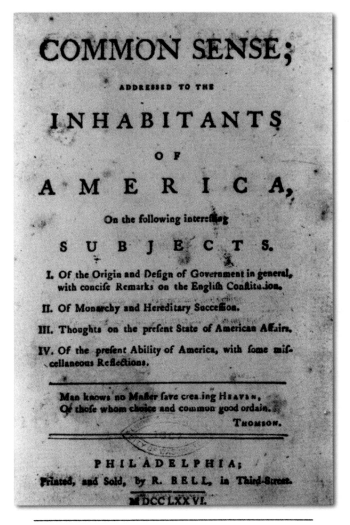

This is the title page of the first edition of Thomas Paine's *Common Sense*. It was printed in 1776, by R. Bell in Philadelphia.

8. The Birth of American Freedom

Thomas Paine realized that getting people to change their beliefs would be difficult. Therefore, he began *Common Sense* by writing, "Perhaps the sentiments contained in the following pages, are not yet sufficiently fashionable to procure them general favor; a long habit of not thinking a thing wrong, gives it a superficial appearance of being right, and raises at first a formidable outcry in defence of custom."

Although change could be painful, Paine knew that Americans would be willing to suffer if the cause was great enough. To convince them of the greatness of their cause, he transformed the colonial struggles between America and Britain into a universal contest over liberty and equality. He wrote, "The cause of America, is in great measure the cause of all mankind." After giving Americans something worth fighting for, Paine then had to convince them that they would need to form a new type of government to establish their freedom.

He started by first examining governments themselves. Paine stated, "Society in every state is a blessing, but government even in its best state is but a necessary evil; in its worst state an intolerable one." Paine said that governments were necessary only because of the "inability of moral virtue to govern the world" and that a government's only function was to provide freedom and security for its people. After stating the function of government, Paine then began to examine monarchy and hereditary succession, thus beginning his revolutionary challenge to the traditional rule of power and wealth.

For twelve years, the leaders of the American resistance movement believed that a corrupt Parliament was attempting to deny them their "rights as Englishmen." Although suspicious of Parliament, the colonists were always loyal to their king, George III. Knowing that he would need to break these bonds of loyalty, Paine showed disrespect and contempt for the traditional institutions of monarchy and hereditary succession. Using examples drawn from both the Bible and history, Paine linked these institutions to tyranny and evil in the world. He wrote, "In short monarchy and succession have laid . . . the world in ashes. 'Tis a form of government which the word of God bears testimony against, and blood will attend it. . . . Of more worth is one honest man to society and in the sight of God, than all the crowned ruffians that ever lived."

Paine basically said that the men who were in power either had seized rule or had gotten it through corruption and war, and then had claimed that God had given their family the right to rule forever. He argued that the

This portrait of King William I of England (1066–1087), William the Conqueror, was engraved by George Vertue.

government of England itself had no legal right to rule. Paine wrote, "[William the Conqueror] landing with an armed banditti, and establishing himself king of England against the consent of the natives, is in plain terms a very paltry rascally original."

Thomas Paine helped to sever the ties of loyalty to the English king by challenging the authority of kings in general. He also reminded Americans of their unique opportunity to shape a new form of government and the importance this present struggle held for the future. Paine wrote, "The sun never shined on a cause of greater worth. It is not the affair of a city, a country, a province, or a kingdom, but of a continent. . . . It is not the concern of a day, a year, or an age; posterity are involved in the contest, and will be more or less affected, even to the end of time, by the proceedings now."

Refuting all arguments for reconciliation, Paine even rejected England as America's mother country:

"Even brutes do not devour their young, nor savages make war upon their families." If government's only purpose was to provide freedom and security, then England had lost its purpose and thereby its power to govern.

Thomas Paine then provided America with a structure of government to replace the British monarchy. Paine proposed having state assemblies, a congress made up of representatives from each state, and an office of president, with term limits. Paine also saw the necessity for a strong, federal government and a constitution guaranteeing individual freedoms. He claimed it was America's natural right to have its own government. Paine also realized that America needed to have one if it wanted help from other nations. As colonies in rebellion, America could expect no help from Europe. Thomas Paine called for a declaration of independence. Paine wrote, "Were a manifesto to be published, and dispatched to foreign courts, setting forth the miseries we have endured, and the peaceable methods we have ineffectually used for redress; declaring, at the same time, that not being able, any longer, to live happily or safely under the cruel disposition of the British court, we had been driven to the necessity of breaking off all connections with her; at the same time, assuring all such courts of our peaceable disposition towards them, and of our desire of entering into trade with them."

By using words common to all social classes, Thomas Paine created a new language of democracy. Making the

> *Abigail Adams was among those impressed by Thomas Paine's* Common Sense. *When her husband, John Adams, sent her a copy, she felt sure that every man and woman in the colonies would have to adopt its sentiments. She promised to pass it along to her friends and family and wrote to John that she hoped it could be "carried speedily into Execution."*

politics of government easy to understand meant greater political and social freedoms for all. This gave Paine widespread appeal among America's working and lower classes. Using the arguments of reason and economic self-interest, Paine also appealed to the colonial elite who were tired of British control, too. Although it would be six months before the Continental Congress signed the Declaration of Independence, the American Revolution for liberty and equality already had begun.

For the next six months, Paine continued to speak and write in support of American independence and republican government. Traveling to New York to visit the American army stationed there, he was the guest of General Charles Lee, who later claimed Paine had "burst forth upon the world like Jove in Thunder." Back in Philadelphia, Thomas Paine wrote a series of articles, later called the Forester Letters, defending American independence and republicanism against pro-British attacks. As the ideas presented by Paine's *Common Sense* filtered through the colonies, state assemblies began to draw up resolutions calling for independence. By early June 1776, Congress was under pressure from the state delegates and appointed a committee to draft a declaration. Although Paine did not hold political office in either the Pennsylvania Assembly or Continental Congress, his influence was felt in both. A friend to the leading radicals in the Pennsylvania Assembly, Paine supported their efforts to change the state constitution, equalize representation, and extend the vote to all tax-paying, white, male adults. Having been the first to call openly for independence, Thomas Paine enjoyed the company and confidence of the leading congressional revolutionaries, including Benjamin Franklin, Thomas Jefferson, and John Adams. These men along with Roger Sherman and Robert Livingston formed the committee that drafted the Declaration of Independence. On July 2, the Pennsylvania delegation to

This is an engraved portrait of General Charles Lee, who lived from 1731 to 1782.

In this undated engraving, Benjamin Franklin, Thomas Jefferson, John Adams, Robert Livingston, and Roger Sherman are shown drafting the Declaration of Independence.

Congress voted for independence. Two days later, after some revisions, they approved the declaration. The thirteen colonies were officially declared free and independent states.

Immediately following this declaration of America's independence, Paine joined the Pennsylvania militia under the command of General Daniel Roberdeau. His unit saw little action. However, what they did see from their station near Perth Amboy, New Jersey, frightened many of the soldiers. The British forces were preparing for the Battle of New York. Gathering on Staten Island, the British army numbered more than thirty thousand troops, including Hessian mercenaries, and their fleet had thirteen thousand sailors and more than one hundred fifty ships anchored offshore. When the enlistment of his unit ended in late September, Paine re-enlisted and served as aide-de-camp to General Nathanael Greene, commander of the American forces at Forts Lee and Washington. Fort Lee, on the Jersey Palisades, guarded the west side of the Hudson River, and Fort Washington, at the northern tip of Manhattan, guarded the east side of the river. The American military command relied on these forts to stop the British from taking control of the Hudson Valley, thereby cutting off New England from the other states.

From high atop the Palisades, Thomas Paine could see the battles of Washington's troops across the river, in Manhattan. Collecting information from military scouting reports for Greene, Paine also served as a war correspondent sending news from the front lines of the war to Philadelphia newspapers. However, by November the outlook for the colonists had worsened. For three months, Washington's army had lost every major battle in New York, including the fight for Fort Washington on the Manhattan side of the Hudson River. Forced to retreat to Fort Lee, Generals Washington and Greene, and Thomas Paine watched from the Palisades as flames streaked the sky above Fort Washington. With victory in sight, British commander General William Howe crossed the Hudson and surprised Washington's troops at Fort Lee. Forced to order a disastrous retreat across the frozen fields of New Jersey, Washington and the American Cause were about to face the Crisis of 1776!

9. Setting the World on Fire

As Washington and his men began their devastating retreat across New Jersey in late fall 1776, the success of the American Cause outlined in *Common Sense* was uncertain. Marching through the half-frozen swamps of New Jersey, Thomas Paine thought about the words that had made American liberty a cause worth fighting for. Unlike the traditional English idea of liberty, which was determined by class and religion, Paine's belief was that each person had the right to liberty, regardless of class, race, or religion. Paine had linked American liberty with equality, "Mankind being originally equals in the order of creation, equality could only be destroyed by some subsequent circumstance." For Paine that circumstance was monarchy, and the means of regaining equality was the American Revolution.

Never before in the history of the world had any nation been founded on the principles of liberty and equality for all people. The American republic that Thomas Paine proposed in *Common Sense* had such widespread appeal because, unlike the British monarchy, which only benefited a small ruling class, America's new republic would represent all classes. By linking liberty to equality, Paine was laying the foundation for the future separation of church and state, the abolition of slavery, and rights for women. Unfortunately, the Americans and their ideals were now in danger of being defeated.

By late November, the Continental army was plagued by desertion, dwindling morale, and inadequate supplies. After many lost battles and retreats, Washington even said, "I think the game will be pretty well up." Realizing that his military efforts were not enough, Thomas Paine turned to his most lethal weapon, his pen. After marching all day, Paine sat by the campfire and wrote all night. In early December, the retreating army made their camp along the Pennsylvania side of the Delaware River. Needing paper and ink, Thomas left camp and marched more than 30 miles (48 km) back to Philadelphia. The city was nearly deserted when he arrived. Fearful of an invasion from British troops, the Continental Congress and most others had left town. Alone in his room, Paine continued to write for the next two weeks, rarely eating or sleeping. He knew his words must reawaken the spirit and promise of American liberty and inspire his fellow Americans to action.

Published on December 19, 1776, Thomas Paine's paper, "The American Crisis," challenged and inspired the American people to continue their fight for liberty:

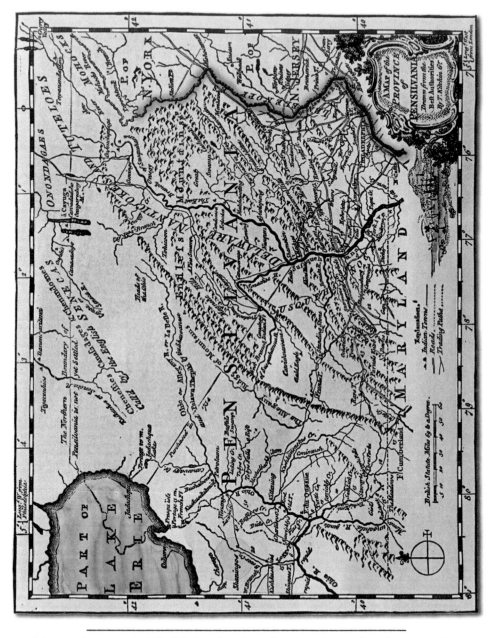

This 1756 map of Philadelphia is a hand-colored woodcut by T. Kitchin.
After several devastating defeats in 1776, the Continental soldiers had
retreated to the Pennsylvania side of the Delaware River, highlighted in
pink. Paine marched to Philadelphia to write "The American Crisis" in
hopes of inspiring the Americans to keep fighting.

"These are the times that try Men's souls. The summer soldier and the sunshine patriot will in this crisis, shrink from the service of their country; but he that stands it now, deserves the love and thanks of man and woman. Tyranny, like hell, is not easily conquered; yet we have this consolation with us, the harder the conflict, the more glorious the triumph. What we obtain too cheap, we esteem too lightly:– Tis dearness only that gives everything its value."

America's response to this crisis, as Paine called it, was immediate. Once again, Thomas Paine's revolutionary prose had inflamed the hearts of the country's patriots. With almost twenty thousand copies printed in just the first edition, "The American Crisis" caused the Continental army's ranks to swell. On Christmas night, 1776, with the American Cause hanging in the balance, Washington's army, inspired by Paine's words, crossed the icy Delaware River and defeated the Hessian troops occupying Trenton, New Jersey. This was the Americans' first great triumph of the war.

In a second Crisis Paper, printed in January 1777, Thomas Paine wrote defiantly to British commander Lord Howe. In the style of a letter, he condemned Britain

Following Spread: This 1851 painting, titled *Washington Crossing the Delaware,* is by Emanuel Gottlieb Leutze. Showing Washington crossing the river to attack the British in New Jersey, this painting is more romantic than historical, but it captures the spirit of the American soldiers just as Thomas Paine's words were able to capture American ideals.

for making war a sport and using senseless violence against India, Africa, and America. In telling Lord Howe that the power of Britain could not defeat the Americans, Paine became the first person to name the new American republic: "The United States of America, will sound as pompously in the world or in history as The Kingdom of Great Britain." During the next six years of the war, Paine published a series of articles that supported the war effort, provided the principles of republican government, and "proposed plans for the strengthening of the American Union."

Thomas Paine's growing influence and importance brought him into close contact with the revolutionary republican leaders in Congress and those in the Pennsylvania Assembly, as well. As the leading republican thinker and writer in America, he was often the focus of the conservative, or pro-British, opposition. Using slander and degrading his class and education, his opponents began a campaign of abuse against him, as seen by the comments of one of Paine's bitterest enemies, Gouverneur Morris. He called Paine nothing better than a "mere adventurer from England, without fortune, without family or connections, ignorant even of grammar."

As a member of New York's ruling class, Morris had little regard for Paine's ideas on equality or the dignity of the common man. As a delegate to the Continental Congress, Morris belonged to a group of political leaders that believed that the common masses could not rule themselves. Fearing mob violence and anarchy, these men considered many of Thomas Paine's ideas about democracy to be a threat to their liberty and property. Yet his powerful prose and commitment to independence forced even his political foes to respect his talent and integrity. In March 1777, Paine was appointed secretary to the Committee of Foreign Affairs. This strategic post gave him unprecedented access to government secrets about foreign alliances. Swearing an oath of allegiance to the new government for the second time (the first being when he joined the Pennsylvania militia), Paine was honored by his role in the new American government.

In September 1777, the British invaded Philadelphia and again the Congress left, this time for York, Pennsylvania. In October, the war effort was unexpectedly successful for the colonists. A victory by General Gates and Benedict Arnold over the British commander General Burgoyne at the Battle of Saratoga all but guaranteed a French alliance with America. With the promise of better times, Paine spent the following winter traveling between General Greene's encampment, his friend Colonel Joseph Kirkbride's home in Bordentown, and Washington's headquarters at Valley Forge. Seeing the condition of the army and hearing rumors of Washington's removal as commander, Paine wrote another Crisis Paper, this time berating General Howe, who was still in control of Philadelphia, and praising Washington for his leadership.

This engraving by Fawel Godfrey shows
British general Burgoyne surrendering to
General Horatio Gates of the Continental army
after the Battle of Saratoga on October 17, 1777.

Although the British left Philadelphia in the summer of 1778, tensions in the city grew as political factions developed between conservatives and liberals within the Revolutionary government. By January 1779, Paine had become involved in the Silas Deane affair. Deane, a lawyer, merchant, and congressional delegate to France, secretly had made arrangements for French military aid to America with congressional approval. However, Congress soon suspected Deane of corruption and war profiteering and recalled him. Proclaiming his innocence,

Silas Deane was minister to France during the Revolutionary War. He lived from 1737 to 1789.

Silas Deane went to the newspapers to defend himself. Outraged by his disloyalty to Congress and having proof of his corruption, Paine publicly exposed Deane for war profiteering. By exposing Deane's corruption, Paine unintentionally threatened other members of Congress with possible exposure, including Deane's powerful friends Robert Morris, John Jay, and Gouverneur Morris. These men waged a campaign of abuse against Paine for exposing corruption in the Continental Congress. These abuses ranged from congressional resolutions criticizing him, led by Gouverneur Morris, to John Jay's calling him an "enemy of the common cause." Never one for "political jockeyship" as he called it, Paine resigned his post in January 1779. Congress's lingering bitterness toward Paine over these public struggles cost him. He would not receive the recognition and compensation that Congress later gave to men who played a far less important role than Paine did in helping to create the American republic. Nevertheless, later that year Paine was

This is a detail from a portrait of John Jay painted by John Trumbull. Jay lived from 1745 to 1829.

This is the original manuscript for the Pennsylvania State Constitution, created in 1776. Thomas Paine helped to write the preamble to the constitution. Pennsylvania's preamble was unique because it was the first in the United States to abolish slavery.

appointed clerk of the Pennsylvania Assembly, where he helped to author the preamble to the Pennsylvania State Constitution.

By 1780, the American war effort was facing another collapse. The fall of Charleston, South Carolina, to the British, Benedict Arnold's treason, and Washington's desperate request for military aid had begun to overwhelm a confused and divided Congress. Once again exhibiting the courage to lead in times of crisis, Thomas Paine took it upon himself to begin a fund that would help finance the war effort. Donating five hundred dollars himself, Paine then approached the wealthy citizens of Philadelphia, including former political foes like Robert Morris. This financial support of the war became the foundation for America's first bank, the Bank of Pennsylvania, and later the Bank of North America. As the struggle for independence raged on, Paine continued to express the principles of republicanism in which the "public good" outweighed the personal interests of a few. In his political essays, letters, and articles, Paine addressed the major issues of the war. From his writings on individual states' rights and the need for a strong federal government in "Public Good" to taxation and military support for the war effort in "The Crisis Extraordinary," Paine never wavered in his fight to keep the Revolution alive. During the winter of 1781, Thomas Paine left his position as clerk to serve as an unofficial envoy to France accompanying John Laurens, the official congressional appointee. Paine was excluded from official participation by a still embittered Congress, even though requesting financial aid from France was an idea taken from "Crisis Extraordinary."

Nevertheless, financing his own trip, Paine accompanied Laurens to France. The trip back to Europe was harrowing. Captained by John Barry, an American naval hero, their ship, the *Alliance,* ran into everything from icebergs and storms to British men-of-war. Finally arriving on March 9, 1781, Paine and Laurens soon joined Benjamin Franklin in Paris. After several months, the French supplied America with

This watercolor by an unknown artist, showing the *U.S.S. Alliance,* was presented to the Naval Academy by John F. Watson in 1860. It is believed to have been painted during the late 1700s. Thomas Paine and John Laurens traveled to France aboard this ship in 1781.

millions of dollars in aid. Upon Lauren's and Paine's return, Congress applauded Laurens's success and ignored Paine's contribution to the mission.

With the American victory at Yorktown, Virginia, on October 19, 1781, the battle for American independence had been won, although peace would not be declared officially until fall 1783. Living in Philadelphia, Paine continued to write in defense of the Revolution, its principles, and the need to strengthen the national government. However, with the war over, Paine's republican politics no longer played as crucial a role in defining the

American Cause. In 1784, Paine was granted a farm in New Rochelle, New York, for services rendered in the "late war." A year later, both Pennsylvania and Congress awarded him money, as well.

Now financially secure, Paine devoted more energy toward his scientific inventions. In winter 1787, Paine displayed a model of his single-span bridge in hopes of building it, but he could not get financial backing either in Philadelphia or New York. Once again he would take Benjamin Franklin's advice and travel abroad, where Franklin suggested he might get funding in France or England. In April 1787, Paine left America for fifteen years, not returning until he had helped set the Old World on fire, just as he had the New World.

This is a photograph of Thomas Paine's cottage in
New Rochelle, New York.

10. A Citizen of the New World

Thomas Paine's fascination with bridges can be traced from his childhood days in Thetford. Living on a small family farm near the lush woodlands surrounding the town, young Thomas must have spent many hours amusing himself, as do most children, with the beauty and simplicity of the natural world. Paine recalled that he got his idea for building his bridge in sections from observing a spider's web: "I naturally supposed that when nature enabled that insect to make a web she taught it the best method of putting it together."

Paine's early interest in science was reinforced by the scientific outlook of the Age of Enlightenment, which followed Newton's discovery of the laws of gravity in the late seventeenth century. This "enlightened" scientific thought focused on how the universal laws of nature applied to society and government. Paine's familiarity with these ideas from the lectures at the Royal Society undoubtedly provided him with a foundation for his nature-based political philosophy in *Common Sense*, "The principle of simplicity of Nature applied to the forms of government shows us that the simplest form is the best. The argument for independence is supported by Nature herself and her principles make the mind of the patriot invincible."

Thomas Paine's interest in building bridges also may have been driven by his perception of bridges as a "human device for mastering nature without disturbing its power or destroying its beauty." If crossing bridges also implies going from the known safety of one side to the unknown of the other side, then building bridges may have symbolized Paine's attempt to bridge the Old World of monarchies to his New World of liberty.

This is the Wearmouth Bridge in Sunderland. The bridge was designed by Thomas Paine and completed in 1796, but replaced in 1929. This drawing was done by G. Balmer and engraved by W. Finden.

This eighteenth-century portrait by an unknown artist portrays
Marquis de Lafayette in his military uniform. Lafayette helped
in America's fight for independence, and also played a vital role in
the French Revolution. Like Paine, he believed that liberty was
universal and not confined to just one country or class system.

Back in Europe, Thomas Paine traveled back and forth between France and England for the next five years. Receiving compliments for his bridge design in both countries, he eventually began to build his bridge in England where he received a government patent for it. Unfortunately, political events interrupted the bridge's construction, and although his design eventually was used to construct a bridge over the Wear River in England, Paine never received money or credit for it. Instead he devoted himself to events in France, where a revolution was brewing that would engage Paine once more in building his "political bridge" to liberty.

Upon Thomas Paine's arrival in France in 1787, he was well received by former acquaintances Thomas Jefferson and Marquis de Lafayette. Paine's political works had made him a celebrity and he enjoyed the company of men like himself who believed that society could be improved through reason and the spread of freedom. Under the burden of taxation in France, popular resentment and anger was growing. Ironically, it was the financial support of America that had created the crisis in France. Though France was a monarchy herself, the French king Louis XVI had supported the American war effort against King George III of England. After the war ended, France found itself facing bankruptcy due to the financial support given to America. Therefore, the king burdened his own people with increased taxes. The people of France were not happy. With no funds in the treasury, the king was forced to call representatives from the three ranks of French society, known as the Estates-General. The aristocracy, or First Estate, the clergy, or Second Estate, and the common people, or Third Estate, met initially to help resolve the financial crisis, but the unrest caused by the crisis allowed the Third Estate to seize control. They restructured the Estates into a National Assembly in June 1789.

On July 14, 1789, after months of increasing food shortages and growing unrest, Parisian mobs stormed the Bastille, an ancient prison that symbolized the oppression of the French monarchy. Uprisings soon spread throughout France as peasant revolts in the countryside forced the government to abolish feudalism and serfdom. This was followed by a proclamation called the *Declaration of the Rights of Man and Citizen*, which established equal rights, religious freedom, and popular sovereignty, or the principle that the people have a right to rule themselves, in France. Impressed by these actions, Paine believed that the principles of the American Revolution were spreading to the Old World, as well. Discouraged by the slow progress in getting his bridge built, Paine was delighted to get an invitation from his friend Lafayette, now commander of the National Guard, to join him in Paris. There he spoke with French and English intellectuals, including Adam Smith, the leading Scottish economist who authored *The Wealth of Nations* in the same year that *Common Sense* was published.

Bearing the key to the Bastille, which Lafayette had asked him to give to Washington, Paine returned to London in March 1790.

When Paine had first come back to England in 1787, he had gone to visit his parents in Thetford. Although his father already had passed away, he spent time with his mother, giving her some money before he left for London. There he had reacquainted himself with the Royal Society whose endorsement he sought for his bridge. Just as in France, Paine's reputation as a freedom fighter in America brought him in contact with powerful political leaders, as well as leading painters and artists.

Now, upon his return from France, he learned that his mother, too, had died. He also learned that Edmund Burke, one of the English political leaders who supported the American Revolution and who had befriended him on his return to England, was preparing an attack on the French Revolution. Fearing that the spread of democracy would create a revolutionary spirit in England as well as France, Burke's *Reflections on the Revolution in France* argued against reason, equality, and revolution. Instead he offered the modern conservative view that tradition and hierarchy were essential to good government, and revolutions caused chaos and tyranny. Calling the common people a "swinish multitude" Burke ridiculed the idea that they were capable of ruling themselves.

Although there were many replies to Burke's work, none captured the public imagination like

This 1791 political cartoon by James Gillray is titled "The Rights of Man, or Tommy Paine, the Little American Tailor, taking the measure of the crown for a new pair of revolution breeches." Gillroy often criticised Paine for his beliefs, but he was a hero to the common people.

Thomas Paine's *Rights of Man*. Although *Rights of Man* was first printed in February 1791, the printer, fearing imprisonment by the government, withdrew the book. Later printed by J. Jordan, *Rights of Man, Part I,* dedicated to George Washington, appeared in London bookstores in March 1791. A huge best-seller, the book defended the French Revolution and its principles of liberty and equality. As in *Common Sense*, Paine argued against monarchy and aristocracy. He wrote: "Hereditary government is an imposition upon mankind, for it is by nature tyranny, since it makes mankind . . . property. Since man has no property in man, every age and generation has the right to be free and act for itself. To presume to rule beyond the grave is the most ridiculous and insolent of all tyrannies."

Then he disagreed with the common belief that war was a necessity of life. He said wars were created by tyrants for their own benefit: "War is the common harvest of all those who participate in the division and expenditure of public money, in all countries. It is the art of conquering at home; the object of it is an increase of revenue; and as revenue cannot be increased without taxes, a pretence must be made for expenditure. In reviewing the history of the English Government, a bystander would declare that taxes were not raised to carry on wars, but that wars were raised to carry on taxes."

Paine ends Part I of the *Rights of Man* with a challenge to the British government to change, or else: "It is not difficult to perceive, that hereditary Government are verging to their decline and that Revolution on the broad basis of national sovereignty, and Government by representation, are making their way in Europe. It would be an act of wisdom to produce Revolutions by wisdom than commit them to convulsions."

In late June 1791, while Paine was back in France, an attempt by the king and queen of France to flee the country failed. At the French border, the royal family was captured and brought back to Paris. With all hopes for a constitutional monarchy dashed, Paine again led the vanguard in proclaiming the need for a republic, a constitution, and an end to monarchy. Persuaded to complete Part II of *Rights of Man* in London, Paine stayed with his friend Clio Rickman. While there he became a leading figure in the political reform groups that were growing in England in response to the revolution across the channel. The British government saw him as a threat, and during the summer, a derogatory biography was written about Thomas Paine by a government employee, under a false name.

Rights of Man, Part II came out in February 1792. Dedicated to Lafayette, the second part began with a memorial to the American Revolution:

> *"The independence of America, considered merely as a separation from England, would have been a matter but of little importance, had it not been accompanied by a revolution in the principles and practice of governments. She made a stand, not for herself only, but for the world, and looked beyond the advantages herself could receive. Freedom had been hunted round the globe; reason was considered as rebellion; and the slavery of fear had made men afraid to think. But such is the irresistible nature of truth, that all it asks,—and all it wants,—is the liberty of appearing. The sun needs no inscription to distinguish him from darkness; and no sooner did the American governments display themselves to the world, than despotism felt a shock and man began to contemplate redress."*

Restating arguments against the tyranny of monarchy and the benefits of democratic republicanism, Paine then stated that class inequality and poverty were also a direct result of this corrupt system. He wrote, "When, in countries that are called civilised, we see age going to the workhouse and youth to the gallows, something must be wrong in the system of government. It would seem, by the exterior appearance of such countries, that all was happiness; but there lies hidden from the eye of common observation, a mass of wretchedness, that has scarcely any other chance, than to expire in poverty or infamy. Its entrance into life is marked with the presage of its fate; and until this is remedied, it is in vain to punish."

Perhaps his boldest arguments, and certainly his most dangerous to the government, were his welfare proposals. Recommending a series of social programs that would create an economic democracy to go along with his political democracy, Paine demanded government relief for the poor and the elderly. Mass education, government jobs, and even funeral expenses for the working poor could all be paid for using government tax dollars collected from the wealthy landowners.

He wrote, "When it shall be said in any country in the world, my poor are happy; neither ignorance nor distress is to be found among them; my jails are empty of prisoners, my streets of beggars; the aged are not in want, the taxes are not oppressive; the rational world is my friend, because I am the friend of its happiness: when these things can be said, then may that country boast its constitution and its government."

In conclusion, Paine wrote, "For my own part, I am fully satisfied that what I am now doing, with an endeavour to conciliate mankind, to render their condition happy, to unite nations that have hitherto been enemies, and to extirpate the horrid practice of war, and break the chains of slavery and oppression is acceptable in his sight, and being the best service I can perform, I act it cheerfully."

With Paine's brilliantly crafted words and logical arguments, both parts of *Rights of Man* soon became England's best-sellers with more than two hundred thousand copies sold within the year. However, the huge publication intensified efforts by the British government to crack down on radicals and reformers. In May 1792, Paine was summoned to appear in court on charges of seditious writings. As an enemy of the state, Paine was under constant surveillance. Government-backed riots soon began over Paine's book, with Paine being burned in effigy. With his trial postponed until December, Paine defiantly continued to write. Then in August, the French government honored him with citizenship, and later the city of Calais elected him to the National Assembly. Leaving England for France in September, Paine never would return to his birthplace, not even for his trial. In December Paine was found guilty and was outlawed in England. The government was fearful of the crowd's response to a guilty verdict for Paine, so the king ordered the militia to London, fortified the Tower, armed it with a cannon, and deployed weapons and troops. Later the government suspended habeas corpus and imprisoned printers found publishing Paine's works.

Arriving in Paris in late September 1792, Thomas Paine found the revolution had changed since he was there last. France was at war, Lafayette had been captured by the Austrians, and violence had begun in the streets of Paris and in the provinces. Still Paine was optimistic that the cause of the people would triumph. Following an

This is Maximilien Robespierre (1758–1794). He was the radical Jacobin leader responsible for the Reign of Terror.

uprising in August 1792, the Assembly passed a decree abolishing monarchy and establishing a French republic. The new French Revolutionary Government called the National Convention appointed Paine to a committee to draft a new constitution. Political differences arose between the moderate Girondin and radical Jacobin factions and soon climaxed over the question of the king's execution. The king already had been found guilty of treason by the convention, but the group was divided on punishment. In one of his greatest acts of courage, Paine challenged the radical leaders of the convention to spare the life of Louis XVI.

This is Jean-Paul Marat (1743–1793), a radical leader during the French Revolution. He was killed by Charlotte Corday.

The Reign of Terror lasted from September 5, 1793, to July 24, 1794. During that time, leaders of the French Revolution enacted laws that severely punished those who were a threat to the revolutionary goals of France. The first set of laws ordered offenders to be put to death whether they were trying to overthrow the government or simply hoarding food. The Committee of Public Safety, a branch of the new government, had wide dictatorial control over France and was led by Maximilien Robespierre. Robespierre became known for his fierce enforcement of the laws that led three hundred thousand people to be jailed and seventeen thousand to be executed in ten months. Eventually there was a harsh backlash against the new laws, and the Reign of Terror ended when Robespierre was arrested and executed.

This is a 1793 French print titled *Mort de Louis Capet 16e du Nom, le 21 Janvier 1793*. It shows the beheading of Louis XVI on January 21, 1793. Though Paine had worked hard to help overthrow the monarchy, he wanted the radical leaders to spare Louis's life. His words did not stop the execution that would signal the beginning of the Reign of Terror.

Facing fierce opposition, Paine infuriated the radical leaders, Robespierre and Marat, when he proposed that the convention abolish the death penalty and exile the king instead. Through his interpreter, Paine proclaimed: "As France has been the first of European nations to abolish royalty, let her also be the first to abolish the punishment of death, and Louis Capet detained in prison till the end of the war, and at that epoch banishment." Paine was unsuccessful in his attempt, and the king was sent to the guillotine on January 21, 1793. Following

THE

AGE OF REASON:

BEING AN INVESTIGATION OF

TRUE AND FABULOUS

THEOLOGY.

BY

THOMAS PAINE,

SECRETARY FOR FOREIGN AFFAIRS TO CONGRESS

IN THE AMERICAN WAR;

AND AUTHOR OF THE WORKS ENTITLED

COMMON SENSE, AND RIGHTS OF MAN,

&c. &c.

PARIS: PRINTED BY BARROIS.

1794.

[SECOND YEAR OF THE FRENCH REPUBLIC.]

This is the title page of the *Age of Reason,* first published in 1794.

King Louis's execution, the Jacobins began their takeover of the convention. Paine soon distanced himself from the daily activities of the assembly and moved outside of Paris to St. Denis, a small suburb. For the rest of the year, Paine stayed there, rarely going into the increasingly violent city of Paris. By the fall of 1793, the French army was in retreat, uprisings were spreading through the provinces, and food riots continued in Paris. Led by the radical leaders Robespierre and Saint-Just, who controlled the Revolutionary Tribunal, the Reign of Terror also had begun. All potential enemies of the Tribunal were prosecuted, imprisoned, and usually executed. They also began an official anti-Christian policy, which wiped out all references to the Christian era, renaming holy days and even the calendar months.

In December 1793, Paine was arrested by the Revolutionary Tribunal as a "foreign conspirator," for being a citizen of England. However, just before he was taken prisoner, he handed his manuscript for *The Age of Reason* to his friend, the American poet Joel Barlow. Written to combat the "dechristianization" policy of the Tribunal, Paine wished to expose the falsity of religious myth while keeping its value structure alive, including the values of morality and humanity. Although raised in a mixed-religious home, Paine considered himself a deist throughout most of his life. Paine believed in a Creator, or first cause, of the universe but denied the Creator's role in everyday human affairs. Paine believed humankind understood God's revelation through reason and the laws of nature. Paine wrote: "I believe in the equality of man; and I believe that religious duties consist in doing justice, loving mercy, and endeavoring to make our fellow creatures happy. I believe in one God, and no more; and I hope for happiness beyond this life. That the moral duty of man consists in imitating the moral goodness and beneficence of God manifested in the creation towards all his creatures and, consequently, that every thing of persecution and revenge between man and man, and every thing of cruelty to animals, is a violation of moral duty."

Sent to the Luxembourg prison through a conspiracy between the French leader of the Terror, Robespierre, and the American minister to France, Gouverneur Morris, Paine suffered greatly there, almost dying from disease. Scheduled to die by the guillotine in July 1794, Paine was spared because a guard mistakenly marked his cell door on the wrong side. Later as the guards came by they saw no chalk mark and passed by his cell. After the new American minister James Monroe officially acknowledged Paine as an American citizen and the leaders of the Terror had met their own fate on the guillotine, Paine was released in November 1794.

Although Thomas Paine spent the next eight years in Paris, he never again took a leadership role in the government. However, Paine continued to write in defense of justice and humanity. In his *Dissertation on the First Principles of Government*, he called for democracy, republican government, and equality of rights. In *Agrarian Justice*, Paine insisted that it was society's moral duty to rid itself of poverty. By 1797, the five officials who were governing France, called the Directory, began a dictatorship. Although heartened by General Napoleon's remark that "A statue of gold should be erected to you in every city of the universe," Paine had begun to lose faith in the revolution. He talked of returning home to America, only hesitating because of the English warships off the coast. Then in 1802, with a cease-fire in effect between France and England, President Thomas Jefferson invited Paine back home to America.

Paine happily accepted the invitation and returned home to America after an absence of fifteen years.

11. Paine's Legacy

Poor Tom Paine! There he lies:
Nobody laughs and nobody cries.
Where he has gone or how he fares
Nobody knows and nobody cares.

Thomas Paine died on June 8, 1809, in Greenwich Village, New York. As this nursery rhyme suggests, due to the campaign waged against his character by church and state, he died with little recognition for the great deeds he had accomplished in the name of America's Cause, a cause that he helped define. Buried on his farm in New Rochelle, New York, his body was disinterred ten years later by William Cobbett and was lost to posterity.

Nevertheless, his political and social philosophy distinguishes him as the world's leading crusader for liberty and democracy. Paine's ideas still inspire those who live under tyranny and oppression to aspire to a world where liberty, democracy, and justice reign.

Thomas Paine devoted himself to championing the rights of the common man. His emphatic belief in the dignity and rights of the individual challenged the traditional authority of king and church and ultimately changed the course of modern history. As his legacy,

Thomas Paine helped create the world's first modern democracy and began a world revolution for the rights of the common man that still continues today! In recognition of his heroic words and deeds, the Thomas Paine Memorial Museum was built in 1925 with the support of Thomas Edison. It stands on the grounds of Paine's former farm in New Rochelle, New York, now part of a national historical site and landmark,

This political cartoon titled "The political champion turned resurrection man," depicts William Cobbett with Thomas Paine's bones. Cobbett, who was an enemy-turned-admirer of Paine's, dug up his bones and brought them to England. It is thought that Cobbett wanted the British people to give Paine a more ceremonious burial, but that he was unable to generate interest and kept Paine's bones in his attic. No one knows exactly what happened to the bones. Some think they were sold, others think they were destroyed or lost. The search for Paine's bones continues today.

including his cottage, monument, and gravesite. Headquarters of the Thomas Paine National Historical Association, the museum provides educational programs, presentations, special events, and tours, which seek to educate the public about the life, times, and works of Thomas Paine. Through this educational awareness the Association endeavors to show that, in Paine's own words,:

WE HAVE IT IN OUR POWER TO
BEGIN THE WORLD OVER AGAIN!

Timeline

1737	Thomas Paine is born in Thetford, England.
1757	Thomas Paine goes to sea as a privateer.
1759	Paine works as a staymaker and marries.
1760	His wife dies in childbirth.
1768	Paine works as an excise collector in Lewes, England, and becomes known as a civic and labor leader.
1772	Paine writes "The Case of the Officers of the Excise." He is later fired from his excise job.
1774	Paine is advised by Benjamin Franklin to seek fortune in America.
1775	Paine begins to write articles for *Pennsylvania Magazine,* dealing with such topics as the abolition of slavery, women's rights, and independence from England.
	The American Revolution begins with the Battle of Lexington and Concord.

1776   Paine publishes *Common Sense* and joins
                  the army as aide to General Greene. He
                  also begins work on his Crisis series.

1777   Paine's Crisis 2 and 3 are published. His
                  popularity growing, Paine is named secre-
                  tary to the Committee of Foreign Affairs.

1778–1779   Paine continues his Crisis series and in
                  his new duties attempts to end corruption
                  and profiteering in the army.

1780   Paine helps to launch the first bank in the
                  new nation.

1781   Paine travels to France in an attempt to
                  raise money for the war effort.

1783   The American Revolution ends.

1783–1786   Paine settles down in Bordentown, New
                  Jersey, and begins to work on several
                  inventions, including a smokeless candle
                  and a bridge without piers. Paine writes
                  on behalf of a strong federal government
                  and a national bank.

1787   Paine leaves for Europe hoping to interest
                  investors in his bridge designs.

1789   French citizens seize the Bastille, a sym-
                  bol of royal power in France, beginning
                  the French Revolution.

1791   In response to Edmund Burke's book *Reflections on the Revolution in France*, an attack on the French Revolution, Paine publishes his defense, *Rights of Man*.

1792   Paine argues against the execution of King Louis XVI of France and calls for an end to capital punishment.

1802   After fifteen years in Europe, Paine returns home, settling in New York. He begins to work on his *Letters to Citizens of the United States*.

1809   Paine dies in New York City and is buried on the farm given to him by the state of New York as a reward for his revolutionary writings and his service in the war.

Glossary

activist (AK-tih-vist) Someone who seeks to change or reform something they believe is wrong in society.

apprentice (uh-PREN-tis) An individual who works without pay in order to learn a skill or craft.

aristocracy (ar-ih-STAH-kreh-see) Government run by a small, privileged class of people.

artisan (AR-tih-zen) An individual who is highly skilled in a particular craft.

boycott (BOY-kaht) An organized effort to refrain from buying goods and services from a company in order to gain a result or change the company's practices.

brutality (broo-TA-luh-tee) An action against someone that shows a lack of feeling or consideration.

derived (di-RYVD) Taken from a specific source.

effigy (EH-fuh-jee) A representation of a hated person.

egalitarian (ih-ga-luh-TER-ee-en) The promotion of the idea that all human beings are equal with respect to social, political, and economic rights.

envoy (ON-voy) A person who speaks for the government of one country in dealings with another country.

escalated (ES-kuh-lay-tid) Increased in amount, volume, number, amount, intensity, or scope.

excise (EK-syz) A kind of tax, manufacture, or sale of a product.

gallows (GA-lohz) A place where criminals are hanged, usually with an upright piece and a crosspiece.

Girondin (juh-RON-din) A group of businessmen in France, in opposition to the Jacobins, who proposed moderate changes in French government during the Revolution.

grievances (GREE-vints-iz) Complaints about practices that one believes to be wrong.

Hessian (HEH-shen) A German soldier who was paid to fight for the British during the American Revolution.

infamy (IN-fuh-mee) An evil reputation for being criminal or brutal.

Jacobin (JA-kuh-bin) The most famous political group during the French Revolution, they sought to protect the social gains made by the peasant class against the French aristocrats. Despite their calls for equality, some members of the organization became known for the worst violence of the French Revolution.

journeyman (JER-nee-man) A worker who has learned a trade from one person but who works for another.

lobbying (LAH-bee-ing) Attempting to influence someone to do something.

man-of-war (man-uv-WOR) A naval warship.

morality (muh-RA-luh-tee) A system of conduct or ideals about what is right and wrong.

oppression (uh-PREH-shun) The unjust exercise of power over another.

persecuted (PER-sih-kyoot-ed) Picked on someone in order to injure him or her.

pillory (PIH-luh-ree) A device, used to publicly punish people, consisting of a wooden frame with holes in which the head and hands can be locked into place.

posterity (pah-STER-uh-tee) All generations to come.

presage (PREH-sij) A warning about something occurring in the future.

prosecuted (PRAH-sih-kyoot-ed) To have taken legal action against someone for the purpose of punishment.

reconciliation (reh-kuhn-sih-lee-AY-shun) A restoration of friendship or harmony to a bad situation.

republicanism (rih-PUH-blih-kuh-nih-zem) The belief that, in a government, power should rest with representatives elected by citizens.

shrewd (SHROOD) Clever, smart.

substantial (suhb-STAN-shul) Something that is not imaginary but real; important or true.

vengeful (VENJ-ful) Seeking to revenge.

Additional Resources

To learn more about Thomas Paine, check out these books and Web sites:

Books

Bliven, Bruce. *The American Revolution* (Landmark Books). New York: Random House, 1987.

Hetherton, Greg. *Revolutionary France: Liberty, Tyranny, and Terror* (Cambridge History Program). London: Cambridge University Press, 1993.

Meltzer, Milton. *Tom Paine: Voice of Revolution*. San Francisco: Franklin Watts, Inc., 1996.

Web Sites

www.kidinfo.com/American_History/American_Revolution.html

www.thomas-paine.com/tpnha/

Bibliography

Conway, Moncure D. *The Writings of Thomas Paine*. New York: G.P. Putnam's Sons, 1894–6.

Foner, Philip. *The Complete Writings of Thomas Paine, 2 vols*. New York: Citadel Press, 1945.

Fructman, Jack Jr. *Thomas Paine, Apostle of Freedom*. New York: Four Wall Eight Windows, 1994.

Kaye, Harvey. *Thomas Paine, Firebrand of the Revolution*. New York: Oxford Press, 2000.

Keane, John. *Tom Paine, A Political Life*. London: Little, Brown and Company, 1995.

Paine, Thomas. "African Slavery in America." Philadelphia: *Pennsylvania Journal*, March 8, 1775.

Paine, Thomas. *The Age of Reason*. Paris: Barras, January 27, 1794.

Paine, Thomas. "The American Crisis." Philadelphia: Pennsylvania Journal, December 19, 1776.

Paine, Thomas. *Common Sense*. Philadelphia: Bradford Edition, February 14, 1776.

Paine, Thomas. *Rights of Man Part Second*. London: J. Jordan, February 16, 1792.

Rickman, Thomas Clio. "Life of Thomas Paine." New York: *Universal Magazine*, December, 1811.

Index

About the Author

Brian McCartin is the director of the Thomas Paine National Historical Association and Museum in New Rochelle, New York. An educator for almost twenty-five years, with a special interest in Thomas Paine, he has developed educational programs and has published articles about this preeminent American founder.

Credits

Photo Credits

Series Design

Laura Murawski

Layout Design

Corinne Jacob

Project Editor

Joanne Randolph

Photo Researcher

Jeffrey Wendt